JUST PROMPT ME

a writer's journal with prompts
book 1

Charlotte Rains Dixon
Nancy Paulson Fox

Dedication

To writers everywhere who follow their
hearts by letting the words flow.

How to Use This Book

You have in front of you a journal of prompts, which are one of the handiest tools for writers available. A prompt can get you—and keep you—writing faster than anything else we know. Prompts are endlessly flexible, creative and useful, which is why we've assembled this book full of them for you. And let us repeat, a prompt will get you writing. And that's the point, right?

When you're a writer (and if you've picked up this book to write in, you most certainly are one, because writers are people who write, period), getting yourself to write is paramount. If you have a choice between doing almost anything and writing, you'll choose writing. If you have a limited time in which to choose an activity, most writers choose writing. Exercise or writing? Writing. Reading a book or writing? Writing. Putting another load of laundry through or writing? Writing. And so on.

You may not have made the bed in days, your home can be in chaos around you, and you've thrown the same clothes on day after day. But at least you're writing. And when you are writing that is all that matters--the writing. And the doing of it. And when you are not writing, that's all that matters, too, the not doing of it.

Writers understand conflict because we live with it every single day--that exquisite tension between writing and not writing. If you're writing, life is good, no matter what else is going on. If you're not writing, you can be the happiest person ever and still a little light is missing from the world.

Thus, getting yourself writing is paramount. But what to do if you can't write for some reason? What if you are blocked? Enter prompts. A prompt is a trigger, an idea-generator, a suggestion, a direct route to your unconscious mind. Usually short, as in a sentence or a phrase (but sometimes as long as a paragraph), a prompt is simply a starting point that will help you subvert the conscious mind's tendency to wring its hands and obsess about writing rather than actually writing.

So, what's the best way to use a prompt? Turn the page and keep reading for some general guidelines.

1. **Choose a prompt**. Don't stop to ponder the prompt. If you stop to think about the prompt, what you think it means, whether you like it or not, or if you should, perhaps, choose another one, then the magic is already gone. And you're just procrastinating! Just pick a prompt and go.

2. **Set a timer**. Fifteen to twenty minutes is good.

3. **Write**. And by this we mean write. Do not stop your hand from moving the entire length of your writing session. Do not stop to think deep thoughts about what you are writing. Do not gaze out the window. Just write. Put words on the page, one after another.

4. **Don't worry about following the meaning of a prompt**. It is just a starting point, a way to get you writing. The prompt may be about the sunrise and you might end up writing about a party that took place in the dark of night. Doesn't matter. The point is to write.

5. **When the timer goes off, stop**. It is a good idea to get up, walk around a little, get a drink of water, give your brain a break. Then you can start in again with another prompt. Or you can go back through the one you just wrote and highlight gems you want to pull out for future use—either as another prompt, or as part of your current writing project. (We've given you some extra space in the back of the book for *notes to self* for this purpose.)

That's all there is to it—so simple and so effective. When you get to the end of this journal, with every page covered with your writing, you'll have a treasure trove of raw material for your work.

So what are you waiting for? Get to it!

You've been prompted: just open the book to any prompt and begin.

Enjoy! Charlotte and Nancy

www.justpromptme.com

What's that awful noise?

The best time to plan a book is while you're doing the dishes.

Agatha Christie

Both gigs were pretty good, but overall he liked being an elf better than a Santa.

The wild, overarching sky.

Angie sat down with a plop, gravity having her way with her. And that was when she knew it was time to ...

The rain fell harder.

What? You did what?

The biggest difference between southerners and northerners is ...

Disaster. The plan was thwarted. What now?

"Oh God, I'm so overwhelmed, things are slipping through the cracks and I'm missing appointments," she said. "Get yourself organized then," he said, reasonably enough. But how?

I try to create sympathy for my characters, then turn the monsters loose.

Stephen King

When in Rome, do as the Romans do, but never, ever...

Getting ready to leave is hard, but coming home and unpacking is even harder.

The most boring thing in the world is when ...

"Off we go, into the wild blue yonder..." Where are we going and why?

God. After all that work and effort, this happens?

She was tired of it all. So tired of the pain, the distraction, and the anxiety. So one day she . . .

Ah, a holiday. All day to relax and do what she wanted. But, oh crap. Then this happened ...

He landed with a thud. And when he looked up at where he had come from, it seemed a very long ways to go. How would he get himself back?

Writing is not necessarily something to be ashamed of, but do it in private and wash your hands afterwards.

Robert A. Heinlein

Write about learning to read.

What would you do if you won the lottery?

Write about a time you woke up.

All this color. It's so overwhelming.

If ever I should leave you, it would be ...

Here's to beginning again ...

But of course you can't do that.

Don't you dare.

Tell the readers a story! Because without a story, you are merely using words to prove you can string them together in logical sentences.

Anne McCaffrey

She sat up quickly. She forgot! She had totally forgotten about it!

Use the words hoar frost, purple, poem and beast in a sentence. Then use that sentence as a prompt.

The best time of day is _____, because
_____, duh.

The lights went out just as she realized her phone was dead.

He hated when he overslept. Because, there was nothing you could do about it-that time was lost. Lost to sleep. So to make sure it never happened, he ...

The fog wafted and drifted around buildings and through streets, masking and silencing everything in its path. So it was a shock when it lifted and ...

Soft and easy.

Afterwards, they ...

> If you can tell stories, create characters, devise incidents, and have sincerity and passion, it doesn't matter a damn how you write.
>
> Somerset Maugham

Nothing better than ...

Please help. Because ...

The bird, the dog and the turtle.

Relentless as ever, he tried to _____
again.

"Well, I never," she said. "I never ..."

"Oh damn, that hill is high," he said, standing at the bottom of it.

Write about what happens when your main character travels. Is he intrepid, an adventurer? Or does he hate leaving home, needing everything to be just as he likes it?

Write about your character experiencing a storm. Is he/she scared or exhilarated? Eager for it to end or happy to let it rage around him/her? Does it energize her or tire him?

> If you write one story, it may be bad; if you write a hundred, you have the odds in your favor.
>
> Edgar Rice Burroughs

The train whistled as it pulled away from the city where she had fallen in love. She sat by the window with her cheek pressed against the glass and watched until she could no longer see the station, or him, standing there waving.

There were a lot of things he would put up with in the world. Rudeness, lateness and laziness for starters. But the one thing he could not abide was incompetence. So when she _____, he _____.

Write an account of an ordinary day in your life.

What a difference a year makes! It had been a year since
_____. She found that hard to believe
because _____.

He should have known better.

The color of morning.

Use the words cat, rain jacket and orchid in a sentence. Now use that sentence as a prompt.

I don't think so.

A blank piece of paper is
God's way of telling us how
hard it is to be God.

Sidney Sheldon

What is your main character's greatest passion?

A young couple is walking their dog (a big, scruffy, black mutt) down the street when they come upon an older man sitting on a bench moaning. "Do you need help? What's wrong?" the young woman asks him. "Oh, do I have a story to tell you."

Write about what your main character does when he's done with work for the day.

Silent night, holy night. All is calm, all is bright. Or is it? What is going on in the dark of this holy eve?

The sun rose higher and higher in the sky, baking the land beneath and all the people in it.

They were eager to get away. But they didn't realize how difficult it would be to leave. How could this happen? Why now?

Write about light, or the lack of it. Every setting has a particular kind of light - bright and sunny, soft and glowy, dark and gray.

Write a scene with your character at her closet, trying to decide what to wear to a party.

> Get it down. Take chances. It may be bad, but it's the only way you can do anything really good.
>
> William Faulkner

Although there was nothing wrong with his leg, he always walked with a cane.

"If I were queen of the world, I would decree that Mondays did not exist," she said. "But then Tuesdays would become Mondays," he said. She shook her head. "I don't care. It just wouldn't be the same." What one thing would you change if you ruled the world?

When he looked outside, all he saw was a sea of

_____.

_____

_____

_____

_____

_____

_____

_____

_____

_____

_____

_____

_____

_____

_____

_____

_____

_____

_____

_____

_____

Me again.

With all our strides in technology, there should be a cure for the common cold.

Cats.

One day when I was out walking, I found a small white bowl, perfectly usable for cereal. Later, on that same walk, I found a small green toy frog that squeaked. Write about something you've found.

Outside it was wet, cold and windy. Inside it was warm and cozy. She snuggled closer to her husband. He looked down at her, his face very serious. "Honey, you're not going to like this, but I have something to tell you." What did he say? How did she react?

> Fiction is about stuff that's screwed up.
>
> Nancy Kress

Who is the love of your main character's life?

You walk into a wine bar that is empty but for two women sitting at a table in the back. Suddenly, their intense conversation ratchets into a loud argument. You can hear every word. Write it all down.

The explosion woke her from a sound sleep.

Every step was painful, but still he walked, on and on. He had to because _____.

The best time of day.

When the party ended ...

They were sad when it was over. So they started up again.

I lost (and found) these things this year: a necklace and a silver fork. Put those words together with the words tape and bus and write a sentence. Now use that sentence as a prompt.

Don't try to figure out what other people want to hear from you; figure out what you have to say. It's the one and only thing you have to offer.

Barbara Kingsolver

The plane rose in the air. She looked out the window at the land-scape below, trying not to grip the armrests quite so hard. Then a noise, like a pop, and the plane shook. "It's turbulence," the man beside her said. But she didn't know whether to believe him or not.

He dealt cards to the four of them playing.   As they picked up
their hands, she said, "This seems like as good a time as any to
tell you." And so, as the game progressed, she told her story.
What did she have to say?

_____

_____

_____

_____

_____

_____

_____

_____

_____

_____

_____

_____

_____

_____

_____

_____

_____

_____

What has your main character had to start over and how many times?

_____

_____

_____

_____

_____

_____

_____

_____

_____

_____

_____

_____

_____

_____

_____

_____

_____

_____

"The horror! The horror! Avert your eyes!" But he couldn't, the scene was just too compelling. Write what he saw and what happened.

The offer that was so good it couldn't be refused, and the terrible things that happened because it was accepted.

Use the words sigh, red, flash and desk in a sentence. Now use that sentence as a prompt.

The sky darkened and lights flashed. It wasn't an electrical storm, though, it was ...

> Writing is its own reward.
>
> Henry Miller

Use the words cheese, red car, and curtain in a sentence. Now use that sentence as a prompt.

What fresh hell is this?

Oh, the glory of it all.

Ha! I don't think so.

It was over. Thank God. She breathed a huge sigh of relief.
But then ...

And suddenly, everything was different. He had stepped into a new world. It was amazing and wonderful ... and a bit scary. What happened?

The wind blew and blew. It blew so hard and so long she thought she'd go crazy from it. And then, all of a sudden, it just stopped.

Lost in space and time.

What she said.

He ran screaming in terror.

Everybody walks past a thousand story ideas every day. The good writers are the ones who see five or six of them. Most people don't see any.

Orson Scott Card

She couldn't wait for him to leave - but she started missing him as soon as he was gone.

They tell me I should never have let anyone know what happened.

She always dreaded parties, and this one was no different. She had to go, no doubt about it, because it was for her boss. Once she got there, she sat in a corner, until ...

Stand up and look out the window. Now write a sentence describing what you see. Use that sentence as a prompt.

After all the shouting died down.

The ways of the world are capricious. Take, for instance ...

And then she discovered the most amazing thing: that most often if she asked for what she wanted, she got it.

Never a dull moment, especially when ...

And then they came to the end . . . or was it?

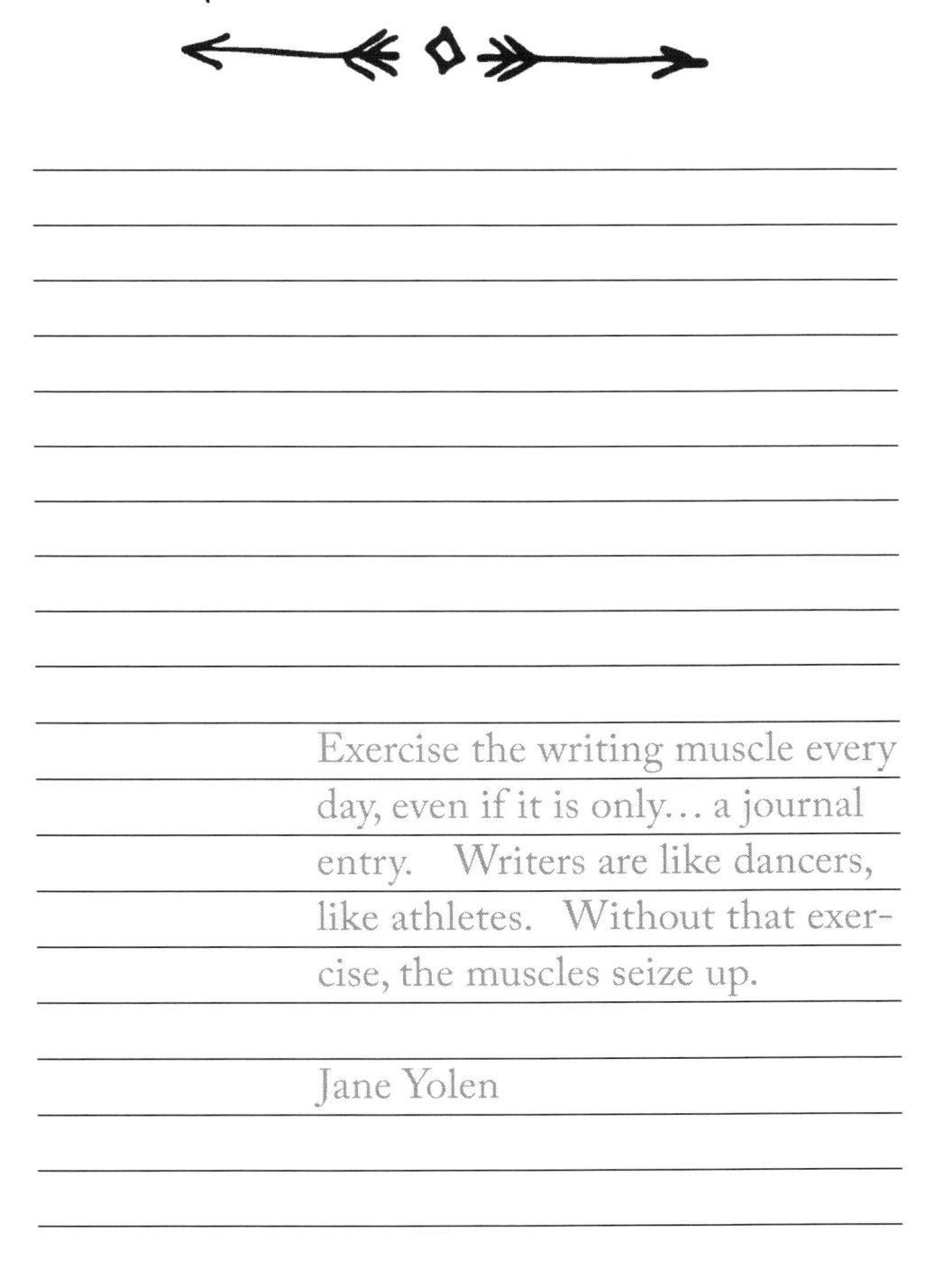

Exercise the writing muscle every day, even if it is only... a journal entry. Writers are like dancers, like athletes. Without that exercise, the muscles seize up.

Jane Yolen

Notes to Self

(For easy reference, fill in these lines with notes or information about your writing you want to remember.)

Notes to Self

Need more room to keep writing?
Here's another set of lines to use . . .

Notes to Self

Still Writing? We hope so!
Here's another set of lines to use . . .

About the Authors

Charlotte Rains Dixon mentors creative writers from passionate to published. Charlotte is a free-lance journalist, ghostwriter, and author. She is Director Emeritus and a current mentor at the Writer's Loft, a certificate writing program at Middle Tennessee State University. Charlotte also teaches privately and hosts writing workshops in the south of France every September. She earned her MFA in creative writing from Spalding University and is the author of a dozen books, including *The Complete Guide to Writing Successful Fundraising Letters*, and *Beautiful America's Oregon Coast*. Her fiction has appeared in *The Trunk*, *Santa Fe Writer's Project*, *Nameless Grace*, and *Somerset Studios* and her articles have been published in *Vogue Knitting*, the *Oregonian*, and *Pology*, to name a few. Her novel, *Emma Jean's Bad Behavior*, was published in 2013.

Charlotte lives in Portland, Oregon. When she isn't writing, she enjoys travel, her family, knitting, popcorn, wine, kitties and pugs-- not necessarily in that order.

Visit her blog at **www.charlotterainsdixon.com**, where you can find all kinds of tips and techniques on writing and creativity with a dash of spirituality.

Nancy Paulson Fox received her B.S. degrees from the University of Washington in Microbiology and Food Science. Nancy started her scientific career testing ice cream quality in a large production facility but transitioned into a career as a legal assistant/office manager. Her creative time is split between making fused glass art and writing, designing and publishing books and journals.

Nancy lives in Kirkland, Washington with her husband. She has two grown children and five grandchildren. Although Nancy grew up as an only child, she is happy to have met Charlotte because in her she has found a "sister from another mother" and is enjoying their collaboration on these *Just Prompt Me* journals.

41336612R00122

Made in the USA
San Bernardino, CA
09 November 2016